A LITTLE GUIDE TO TATTOOS

A LITTLE GUIDE TO TATTOOS

VERENA HUTTER

ILLUSTRATED BY ERIC HINKLEY

RP MINIS

PHILADELPHIA

RP Minis®
Hachette Book Group
1290 Avenue of the Americas, New York, NY 10104
www.runningpress.com
@Running_Press

First Edition: May 2024

Published by RP Minis, an imprint of Hachette Book Group, Inc. The RP Minis name and logo is a registered trademark of Hachette Book Group, Inc.

Running Press books may be purchased in bulk for business, educational, or promotional use. For more information, please contact your local bookseller or the Hachette Book Group Special Markets Department at Special.Markets@hbgusa.com.

Design by Jenna McBride.

ISBN: 978-0-7624-8598-7

THE RISE OF AMERICAN TRADITIONAL STYLE

American traditional style tattoos are characterized by big, bold outlines made with a liner with multiple needles, heavy black shading, and a limited color palette—mainly the primary colors. The imagery of these tattoos is deeply influenced by the real-world experiences of those who were tattooed in the United States in the late 19th to early 20th centuries: sailors, soldiers, and show people of the circuses

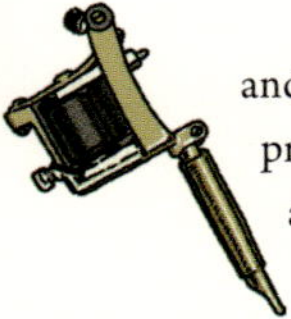

and sideshows. Tattoo artists practicing this style know they are part of a long tradition of misfits, craftspeople, storytellers, artists, and visionaries—those on the fringes of society, but still a vital part of it.

The Civil War (1861–1865) introduced the concept of tattoos to many U.S. households. Many soldiers on both sides had their names, their regiments, or important symbols tattooed on themselves so that they could be identified in case of their death, when uniforms and stripes could get lost.

Tattoos at the time were still done by hand and with either black or vermillion ink. Martin Hildebrandt, who claimed that he had tattooed thousands during the Civil War, opened the first tattoo shop in the United States as early as 1859.

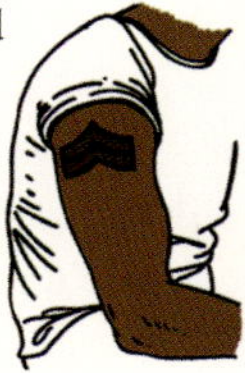

The European immigration wave (1880–1920s) ushered in a new age for tattooing. The Bowery, an area in the Lower East Side of Manhattan, became a lowbrow amusement area, where Hildebrandt and other tattooers set up shop. And when Samuel O'Reilly, another legendary Bowery tattooer, patented his tattoo machine in 1891, the craft was further catapulted into a new era. Tattooers now posted images of their designs, called "flash," in the windows or the doors of their shops as advertisement for their services.

With its wild history, stark imagery, strong symbolism, and larger-than-life characters, American traditional style will always be a beloved mainstay of tattooing culture.

TATTOO SYMBOLISM

American traditional tattoos are rooted in the everyday experiences of their wearers. If you were a sailor, getting a tattoo with an anchor or a sailing ship reflected your life. With an anchor, for example, the tattoo expresses its wearer's hope for stability. A lot of the tattoos are also superstitious; they are symbols of luck and possibility. At a time when life at sea or in the military was full of dangers, a little extra luck could go a long way for an individual. While these traditional tattoos may look simplistic at first glance, one of their most fascinating qualities is their versatility.

SWALLOWS

High in the sky, birds stand for freedom, and their cheery presence is uplifting. For sailors, swallows or bluebirds also were a literal symbol of hope, as they indicated that land was near. Swallows and other migratory birds signify good luck on travels, as they always return home no matter how far away they wander. On a more somber note, some also believe that birds carry the soul of a deceased home.

Their positive and cheerful symbolism is also reflected in the strong, happy tattoo colors, such as blue and red or yellow. In some seafaring circles, a swallow tattoo meant that the sailor had traveled 5,000 nautical miles; two swallow tattoos—often placed on opposite shoulders—meant 10,000 nautical miles of travel.

The combination of a swallow and anchor is also a beautiful way to signal your steadfast nature, and it can work like a protective charm; regardless of how stormy the waves of life are, you're undeterred.

OCTOPI

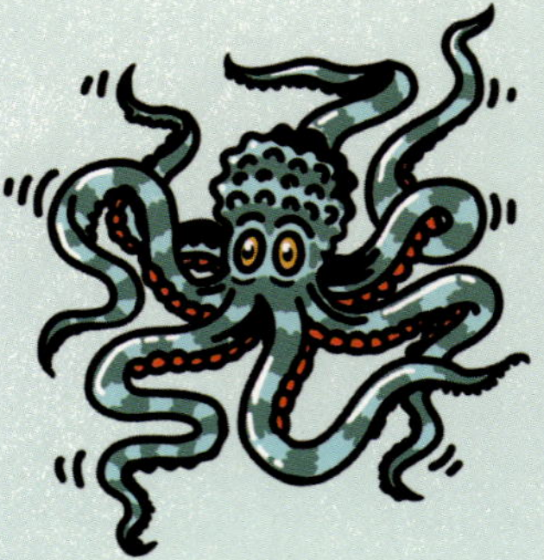

Octopi are some of the most enigmatic creatures of the sea. Living deep underwater, they usually avoid humans, which is why they are such a sensation when they show up. Their squishy shape and eight arms have given rise to many imagined creatures of the sea, such as the Kraken, a mythical sea monster off the coast of Norway.

Whether the octopus tattoo is inspired by myth or reality is impossible to trace. Some people will get an octopus tattoo because they love the intelligence of these creatures. Because some octopi kill their prey by releasing venom from their arms, octopi tattoos can also be a warning and a sign that you mean business. Dramatic tattoos, such as an octopus wrapped around an anchor, can express duality—staying grounded and strong while being curious and putting out feelers in different directions.

SHARKS

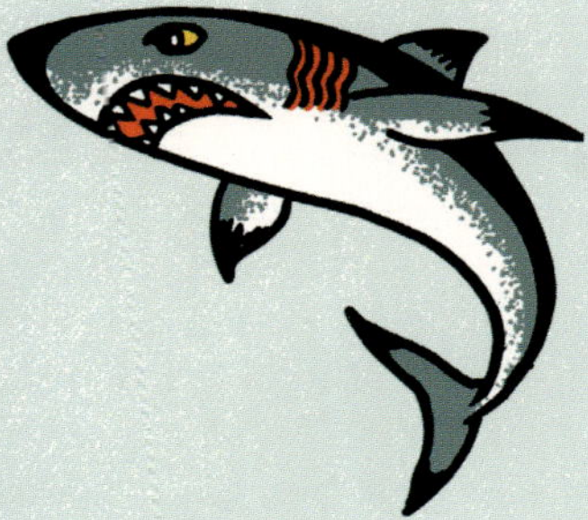

Sharks can be found in every ocean and come in every size. There are over 500 species of shark, some of which are apex predators. Sharks play an important role in Hawaiian and Samoan cultures, where they can be an embodiment of the ancestors' spirit. In modern popular culture, sharks unfortunately have been portrayed negatively, such as in horror films or in a children's song about a family of sharks that shall not be named.

Shark tattoos usually feature the shark emerging from the water, displaying its sharp teeth. Sharks are quick, move elegantly, and as efficient killing machines, they are a fearsome, yet formidable foe. A shark tattoo affirms its wearer will stand their ground; it's eat or get eaten. For sailors, shark tattoos were about the daily danger that their lives entailed and symbolized facing their fears.

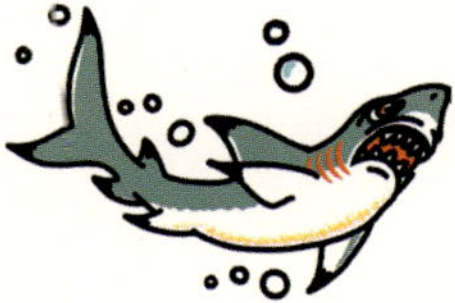

BOXERS

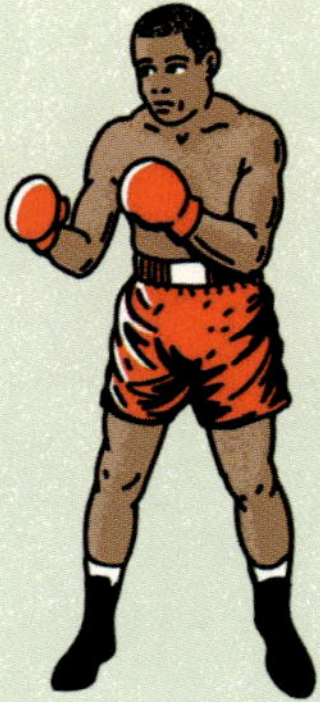

While brawling is as old as time, the first recorded rules for boxing originated with the Marquess of Queensberry in 1867. Because of the sport's strict adherence to rules, the respect for one's opponents, and the hard training boxers undergo—as the montages in *Rocky IV* taught us—boxing is seen as a gentlemanly endeavor.

The boxer tattoo reflects that quality. Depicted in 19th-century style, with a figure with parted hair, a moustache, sometimes a black eye and/or tattoos, the boxer is in many ways the male equivalent to the pinup girl. As an idealized version of masculinity, the boxer is a tattoo for those who face the struggles of life in a fair, stoic, and disciplined manner.

The boxer tattoo symbolizes courage, fierceness, and self-control. Whatever life throws at you, you know you can take and land a punch.

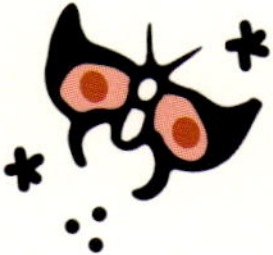

ROSES

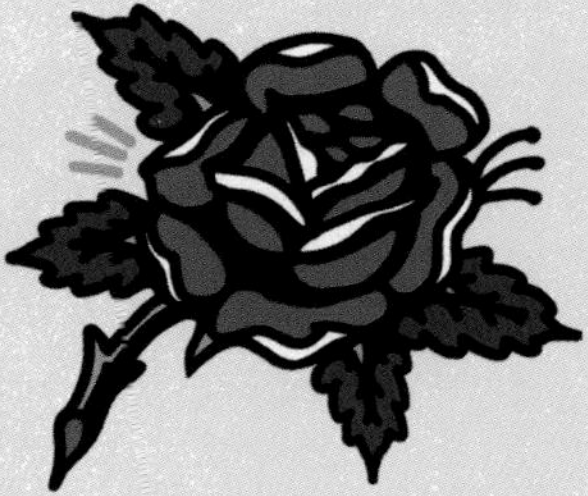

Roses have often been associated with deities, such as the goddess Venus for Romans or the Virgin Mary for Catholic Christians. No matter who has used the rose as a symbol, its meaning has stayed fairly constant—love, beauty, and passion.

The color of the rose also affects its meaning. To celebrate friendship, people get matching yellow rose tattoos. Pink rose tattoos are lighter in color than the traditional red, and convey joy, friendship, and femininity. Another way to modify your design is to add a thorny stem to the red rose, symbolizing not only love and devotion, but also the possibility of pain. A dagger and a rose can tell a tale of love and betrayal, and a skull and a rose can be a promise—that your love only ends with death—or a warning.

MERMAIDS

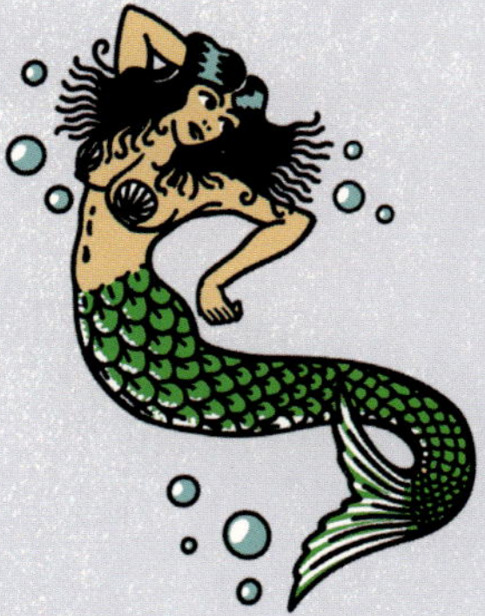

Throughout history, sightings of mermaids have been reported, most famously by Christopher Columbus—though most historians agree he probably saw manatees, from far, far away. For sailors, the mermaid tattoo averted bad luck and protected their journeys. The traditional mermaid tattoo, which had a resurgence thanks to Sailor Jerry, bears resemblance to the pinup, having her breasts covered by long locks of hair or seashells, but not obscuring her seductive nature.

Their half-human, half-fish form embodies the twofold symbolism of the tattoo: According to legend, mermaids use their feminine beauty and siren song to lure sailors into storms or drag them underwater, a warning that beauty and perdition sometimes come together. In other myths and stories however, mermaids warn travelers of danger. Neither completely good nor totally bad, mermaids are more than meets the eye, and whether you love them or not, they demand your respect.

LIGHTHOUSES

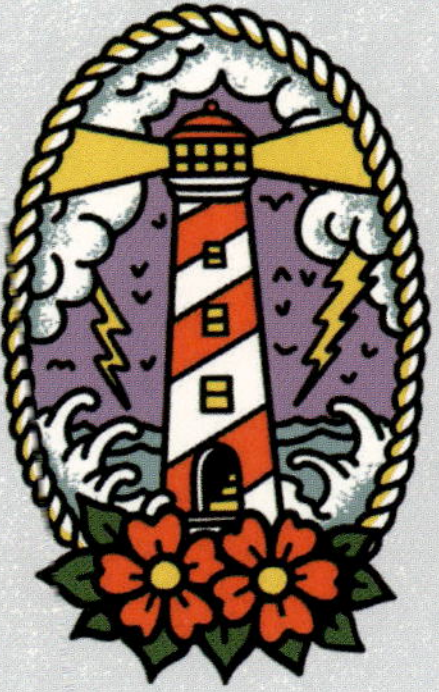

One of the oldest symbols of guidance and hope, lighthouses mark dangerous coastlines, warn of storms, and safely lead ships into harbors. As a tattoo, the lighthouse expressed the wish and hope to return home safely for sailors and servicepeople. A lighthouse guides ships and travelers through the night and choppy waters; a tattoo of one may act as a symbol of hope if you have gone through dark times.

Connected to the earth, withstanding wind and weather, the lighthouse also symbolizes quiet strength and leadership. It will not budge. If those are qualities you possess—or desire—a lighthouse tattoo, perhaps embroiled in a storm or with crashing waves, is a powerful way to show this.

You may want to combine the lighthouse tattoo with a beach sunset. A colorful, especially positive tattoo, it offers the hope and guidance of the lighthouse with the beach sunset's promise of a new day.

SAILING SHIPS

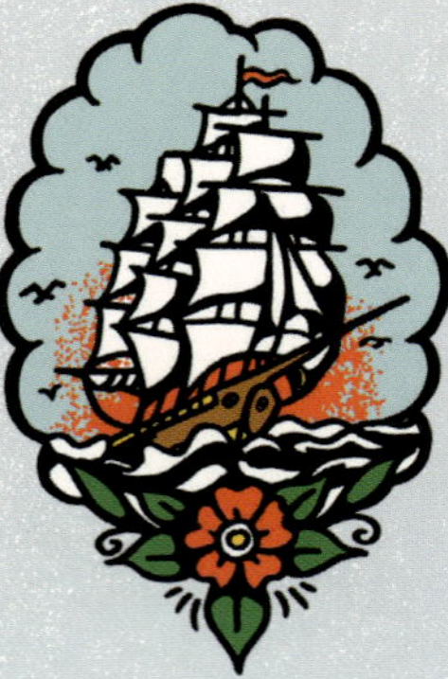

To a sailor, the sailing ship is the home away from home, symbol of their lives' transience—they belong to neither the land nor the sea. It is also a symbol of adventure. From fighting the elements to bad morale and from rotten food to pirates, there were—and are!—plenty of dangers associated with seafaring. The sailing ship is a protective tattoo for sailors hoping for a safe journey, especially when connected to other good luck symbols, for example, if it is inside a horseshoe. Sporting a sailing ship may also tell others that there is more to you than just the surface—the ship may be alone at sea, but there are a lot of people on it that make it work.

Some of the most famous sailing ship flash were created by Sailor Jerry, who ensured that his art was technically accurate down to the last detail.